Dwelling in Possibility

*40 Days of the Spacious,
Brilliant Essence of Me*

LINDA VILLEGAS BREMER

PAGE PUBLISHING, INC.
Conneaut Lake, PA

First originally published by Page Publishing 2020

ISBN 978-1-64584-757-1 (pbk)
ISBN 978-1-64584-756-4 (digital)

Printed in the United States of America

CONTENTS

ACKNOWLEDGMENT

When I reflect on my parents' diverse contributions, I appreciate their opening horizons of promise. They demonstrated amazing results—materially and spiritually. Their triumphs were motivating.

I am grateful for the contributions of Emily Dickenson, Ernest Holmes, Joe Dispenza, Context International, and many others.

These teachers, scientists and "imaginationists" have opened us up to the access of possibility.

INTRODUCTION

This 40-day journey is one of discovery—of remembering who we are.

It's an opportunity for each of us to spend 40 days strengthening our belief in all things possible.

Whether you are seeking greater satisfaction in career, relationships, health, or wealth—the possibility to create your desired results is throbbing through you, **as** you, right now. It is the same impulse as the Divine Intelligence that propels the stars.

I invite you to spend time reflecting and connecting again and again with the life-giving energy that manifests all that is and all that will be. I have embedded questions in the daily reflections. You may be moved to jot down your ideas, your responses, your "aha's."

Ernest Holmes is my hero. He founded the International Religious Science movement and wrote *The Science of Mind* and numerous other books on metaphysics. Holmes's *Science of Mind* teaching, recognized today as one of the leading viewpoints in modern metaphysics, is a spiritual philosophy that has brought to people around the world a working cosmology—a sense of their relationship to Divine Mind and their place in the Universe—and a positive, supportive approach to daily living.

He was a troubadour of the love story connecting spirit and science—of how spiritual principles were reflected in the scientific thought of his day. Or was it how scientific thought bore out spiritual principles? I am fascinated by the intertwining dynamics of *Science of Mind*.

Decades later, we have new scientific findings that reinforce the philosophy of science of mind, modern metaphysics, New Thought. One definition of New Thought describes it as a philosophy that promotes the ideas that *Infinite Intelligence*, is everywhere; spirit is the totality of real things; true human selfhood is divine; and divine thought is a force for good.

Positive psychology is a recent branch of psychology affirming that positive human functioning can build thriving individuals, families, and communities, affirming the importance of finding and nurturing genius and talent. It supports the idea that cultivating happiness is a cornerstone for effective results in life.

Neuroscience has made great strides in how the brain works and how the "mind" comes to be. My favorite topic is the functioning of mirror neurons. It is believed that the mirror neuron system forms the basis for empathy—possibly defining self-awareness and other-person-awareness—truly creating a oneness of being.

String theory is the first theory of physics that tries to explain everything. What does it mean to explain everything? We would know how the universe began and where it is going. A theory of everything would explain everything we feel, see, or measure. We would understand all the forces and all types of matter. We would know what is most basic, and how everything else is composed of these basic parts. It postulates that there are eleven dimensions—not just the four with which we are comfortable. Are we a hologram?

And what about the Higgs boson? It is also called the "God" particle. It is said that the Higgs boson essentially holds the universe together. It gives particles mass, which allows them to bind together and form things, like stars and planets, and you and me. These Higgs boson particles make up an invisible force throughout the universe called a Higgs field. Without it, the universe, as we know it, could not exist.

Modern science strengthens the ideas presented by Ernest Holmes, the ideas he synthesized from common themes across spiritual teachings. The mysteries of the Universe that continue to be revealed are spellbinding. Through Holmes's writings, I have adopted practices that have led to greater satisfaction in my life. If you too are practicing these tenets of ancient wisdom, let's celebrate Holmes—a New Thought pathfinder!

If you are new to New Thought philosophy, I celebrate your interest in exploring new ways of bringing more of life's good into your life.

I like to use the workings of a GPS (global positioning system) as a metaphor to describe how our thoughts create results, how we each manifest our reality on this physical plane.

In a standard GPS:

- First, maps have to be loaded into the device so that no matter where we are, we can navigate our way to where we need to be. These maps are updated regularly to reflect changing conditions.
- Second, we need a very specific destination; if we ask for South Cedar instead of North Cedar, we will miss the mark.

- Third, we pay attention to feedback that says whether we are on course or whether we need to adapt.

So it is that our thoughts, our brains, produce outcomes.

- First, maps are loaded into our brains. We call these maps our attitudes and beliefs. How are beliefs created? Neuroscientists tell us that as we take in information, our brain interprets and manipulates it to make sense of it. This interpretation takes place using information already stored to screen this new data and decide how to integrate it. The more we think that something is true, the stronger the neural pathways and the stronger our beliefs. We are in charge of those maps. This is great news! Our brains can be rewired! We can change the beliefs that don't serve us by affirming beliefs that support our highest good. We can update our personal maps and take our thoughts on new glorious journeys.
- Second, we need to give our brain a specific destination for our desire. If we don't give our brains a specific goal, we will drift from one experience to another. When we focus, we synchronize with the divine creative power, and we are on our way to our destination, generating that which is important to us. We start from where we are.
- Third, by paying attention to our feelings, emotions, and what we are manifesting, we get feedback on whether we are on track or not. It's important to be self-aware and listen to that *Divine Discontent*—anxiety, depression, fear, confusion…

Holmes has said, "To live in this consciousness of unity we have to release and let go of the past. This is part of changing our thinking so that we can change the way we experience our lives. Yes, the disappointments of the past serve us; they create within us a *Divine Discontent* that moves us forward. *Divine Discontent* is a creative urge. Most of us, will after a while at least, make a change if something makes us chronically miserable, but often we find that we have tolerated inconveniences, lack of fulfillment and circumstances that somehow miss the mark. We might not at first make an effective change, but we will make an effort when things are truly difficult. To have a great life, we have to wake up and quit tolerating the mediocre and unfulfilling. Yes, there are things that are inconsequential. The light of awareness and spiritual practice will distinguish the difference between these."

What I appreciate so much about this study is that regardless of where I am in life, regardless of conditions, I can choose again. I can then allow the universe of possibility to manifest through me, as me. Let's not wait for the truly difficult. Let's start today.

I have a friend who is a skeptic and doesn't know what to make of these teachings. She says, "To me, life is just about Physics." I agree with her. And yet I know that scientists who have discovered the principles of physics are simply discovering something that was already there. They are simply explaining extraordinary phenomena already present. I don't have to know the answer. I am certain that one hundred years from now, whoever is on the planet then, will look back at this age and wonder how we ever accomplished what we did with our primitive knowledge. There is much we still have yet to discover about the principles of how the universal life energy works.

I once took classes at Context International. I learned about the Context Window. I learned that my opinions, attitudes and beliefs create my context. They create a window through which I see the world. They create my judgments, my thoughts. And through Ernest Holmes's work and Joe Dispenza's neuroscience lessons, I also learned: Thoughts create my reality.

Thoughts + Feelings → Actions → Results

Thoughts give rise to actions. The actions I take, or don't take, create my results.

I am reminded of Pascal's Wager. It posits that humans all bet with their lives either that God exists or does not exist. Given the possibility that God actually does exist and assuming the infinite gain or loss associated with belief in God or with unbelief, a rational person should live as though God exists and seek to believe in God. (If God exists, I win. If God *doesn't* exist, I still win.)

Einstein has been quoted as saying, "There are only 2 ways to live life. One is as though nothing is a miracle. The other as though everything is."

I'm into winning and supporting those around me to win too! I'm asking you to live as if you **can** manifest your heart's desire. I invite you to see the potential that awaits your focus and deliberate intention. There is nothing to lose and everything to gain.

Much has been made of the Law of Attraction. It states that "like attracts like." Let's have fun. Let's play. Some call it the Law of Radiation. Radiate what you like. At the very least, I predict you'll be feeling great!

Regarding the word "God"—just remember, that whatever you name that Universal Lifegiving Energy, is your call. In the Star Wars movies, they call it "The Force." You decide. Let's let go of limitations.

DAY 1

This world is but a canvas to our imagination.
—*Henry David Thoreau*

The universal Mind contains all knowledge. It is the potential ultimate of all things. To it, all things are possible.
—*Ernest Holmes*

I love Thoreau's image of "a canvas to our imagination." I get the feeling that my imagination is a dynamic energy waiting to express and that the canvas is calling. Which it is!

As I look upon this day…

What's the joy in this day?

What strengthens me?

Am I bringing forth the best of me?

What picture will I paint on this glorious once-in-a-lifetime canvas I call today?

Knowing that I am one with Universal Mind—that infinite pool of divine intelligence—I open myself up to listening to my heart's desire. I am the vessel for possibility.

As I ponder the following, I give myself freedom to let my thoughts flow uncensored.

Who am I here to be?

What are my strengths?

What are my desires?

What am I here to do?

When I reflect on my heroes, what do I appreciate about what they do?

If money were no object, what would I be doing?

I accept the gifts of the Universe with open arms.

I am cocreating vivid, life-affirming spiritual art.

I look within to begin.

I live in the wonderful world of possibility.

DAY 2

*All positive change in the world comes from our ideas of what
we believe is possible.*

—Alexandra Jamieson

*We are all thinking, willing, knowing, conscious centers of
Life. We are surrounded by, immersed in, and there is flowing
through us a creative something…call it what you will.*

—Ernest Holmes

What do I believe is possible?
Do I judge what is happening in the present a measure of what I can do?
My comfort zone is familiar. I feel safe, protected, competent. That's its job.
Have I turned over all my prospects to the status quo? What am I to do?
My personal expression of Universal potential is in me, waiting for me to
take a new step.
Isn't it interesting?
As I reflect on where I am, I realize that today I am in a different place from
where I started.
I *have* taken risks. Small ones. Big ones. And I made it!
At times, I was uncomfortable.
In the end, I stretched. I adapted. I improvised. I evolved my perspective.
My comfort zone expanded. I can do it again!
By expanding my horizons, I create opportunity.
So I say, "Yes!"
I'm ready to run to the edge of my comfort zone.
And step into my enriched future with zest.

**I have the power of the entire Universe in me—
breathing, thinking, and moving as me.**

DAY 3

Now is the time. Needs are great, but your possibilities are greater.

—Bill Blackman

Just keep right on knocking at the doorway of your consciousness until every "no" becomes a "yes," every negation an affirmation, every fear a faith.

—Ernest Holmes

Now. This minute. Today.

What am I up to?

Am I allowing my perceived limited sense of what I can be, do, and have to define me?

To overwhelm me?

I look outside, and I see potential expressing spontaneously and effortlessly—
in the birds, the trees, the clouds, the ants.

Everywhere I turn, I see splendor. I see power.

I see the rhythm of life constantly manifesting something new.

I am one with that energy that pulses in the stars and propels the galaxies.

My possibilities are, indeed, greater than I can imagine.

I welcome my recognition of the power that flows through me, as me.

What steps am I taking to learn more about my consciousness?

Do I recognize those times when I tell myself, "No?"

Do I acknowledge myself when I tell myself, "Yes?"

Am I steeped in faith, knowing that all my dreams are possible?

I feel my passion, and it boosts me to greater and greater heights.

I am happy, creative, abundant, and fulfilled.

DAY 4

The power of imagination makes us infinite.

—John Muir

True imagination is not fanciful daydreaming; it is fire from heaven.

—Ernest Holmes

I used to think of imagination as pondering the impossible.

Some would say imagination is the ability to form images and ideas in the mind, especially of things never seen or experienced directly. I used to see it as a skill.

Now I know that imagination is inherent in my being.

It is a divine essence that allowed the "baby me" to take that first step and learn to walk.

It is an inner drive to create a brand-new day, a brand-new way.

Wouldn't it be great if…? What if I…? What if…?

As I contemplate our human expression of time, it seems otherworldly that the energy that created **everything** burst forth in a nanosecond. Or was that a picosecond? An attosecond?

In that unfathomable twinkling of an instant, everything came to be.

Science tells us that we are not creating new energy.

All that ever will be, through infinity, was created inexplicably at once.

I was born in that moment.

Universal Imagination brought forth all that I see.

My human form took billion of years to emerge.

I am the fire of heaven! I am possibility made flesh. I flex in stepping into possibility.

I begin again and again to reinvent myself daily.

DAY 5

People get what they want in life when they reach the point at which they can see themselves having what they seek.
—Thomas D. Willhite

Life is a mirror and will reflect back to the thinker what he thinks into it.

—Ernest Holmes

"Life is a mirror."
I have what I want. Really? Yes! Really.
The results in my life are a confirmation of what I want.
Do I have love in my life? What about wealth? My livelihood?
My living space? My friends?
Do I judge what I do have? Is it good? Is it bad? Does it look the way I want it to look?
When I watch a baseball game and there's a close call at home plate, it seems as if time stands still and the spectators hold their breath, waiting for the umpire's call.
"Safe."
"Out."
I find that I am often my life's umpire.
I find I call myself "Out," "Safe," "Bad," "Good," "Not enough."
In this moment, I let go of judgments, situations, and things simply and neutrally are.
Regardless of appearances, I choose to see each moment as leading to my greater unfoldment.
I am One with all that is.
My life's conditions simply are.
Instead of issuing verdicts, I reflect on what's important to me.
Once I have clarity, I can crystallize my thought—my powerful, creative, ingenious, and inspired thought. I give myself permission to receive, to cocreate, to manifest.

**I can be, do, and have anything I want, *how*
I want. All it takes is a thought.**

DAY 6

Nothing is impossible; the word itself says 'I'm possible'!
—Audrey Hepburn

Prepare your mind to receive the best that life has to offer.
—Ernest Holmes

There was a time when flying was impossible for humans.

I'm still mystified that someone had the idea that sound could travel through a medium.

I can talk to my friends thousands of miles away, as if they were in the same room.

It feels like magic—a conjurer's trick.

"I M" Possible.

I Am Possible.

Where have I held an idea that something is impossible for me?

In my career/vocation? My body? My prosperity? In love?

I believe in the abundance that is mine.

I believe that the Power of the Universe flows through me, as me.

I give up my thoughts of impossible.

These illusions float away and dissolve into the nothingness, from which they arose.

I know, with certainty, that I am one with the energy of this elegant, divine universe.

I am prepared! I am ready, willing, and available to receive the best life has to offer.

I live my life centered in joy!

I approve of myself. I love myself.

I give thanks for all that I am and all that I am becoming.

I am open to endless possibilities! Yowza!

DAY 7

Stop thinking in terms of limitations and start thinking in terms of possibilities.

—Terry Josephson

We are not depending on a reed shaken by the wind, but on the Principle of Life Itself, for all that we have or ever shall need. It is not some Power, or a great Power, it is all power.

—Ernest Holmes

Every thought flowing through my mind has power. **Is** power.

Not only is my brain sifting and sorting, modifying, and manipulating information—these thoughts are creating my beliefs.

Everything I see was first a thought. Every action I take was first a thought. The brain operates with a cognitive imperative. It is either processing conscious thoughts or unconscious thoughts. I want to fill up my mind with conscious uplifting thoughts that can find a permanent home in me.

I believe that every thought is a prayer. Too often, prayer is defined as an entreaty, appeal, or plea.

I like Ernest Holmes's framework of affirmative prayer known as a treatment. It provides for clarity of focus of my desire and a knowing that it is done unto me as I believe.

It involves a five-step process that harnesses the creative process of consciousness. I start with a **Recognition** that there is one Source of all that is—that divine energy of creation. I **Unify** with that Source, knowing that all in the universe *is* energy and I am one with that energy flow, one with Source. I state what I want to **Realize** in language that asserts that it is already mine, for my thoughts are Power. I give **Thanks**—expressing my gratitude that this is already done. And I **Release** it to that divine creative process to do its work for me. I know that this is so, and so it is.

I love that composition. It supports me in having a paradigm that works in my favor.

It is my tool for generating more and more thoughts that work for my highest good.

Isn't this the best yet?

I believe in the creative power of my thoughts and my words.

DAY 8

*Our imagination is the only limit to what we can hope to
have in the future.*

— *Charles F. Kettering*

*I live in the faith that there is a Presence and Power greater
than I am that nurtures and supports me in ways I could not
even imagine. I know that this Presence is All knowing and
All Power and is Always right where I am.*

— *Ernest Holmes*

All that keeps the planets and stars in motion is a sea of potential.
I am swimming in those waters.
More important, everything that exists, everything that is yet to be, is an
individualization of that Source.
I am the creative process in motion.
I am universal energy in form.
Just as the waves on the ocean crest, flourish, and demonstrate their mag-
nificence…so do I.
I am nurtured by Divine Mind.
I am encouraged by the intrinsic life essences of creativity and resourcefulness.
How do I honor my divinity?
Do I take the time to see the divine in those around me?
Do I release that which no longer serves me?
Do I let others support me?
I believe in me.
I am headed for glory.

**I put my faith in my inner guidance, and the
Universal Life Force lights my path.**

DAY 9

I skate to where the puck is going to be, not where it has been.
—Wayne Gretzky

Never limit your view of life by any past experience.
—Ernest Holmes

On this life's journey, I realize that my brain is the "air traffic controller" of all the information flowing across billions of neurons and throughout the distributed intelligence centers in my body. My brain is a recordkeeper. It uses the experiences of the past to assess whether something worked before or not. It is vigilant.

This data bank is limited. It has stored data based on "best guess"—okay, maybe based on "best interpolations of data and sensory information." It assimilates what I perceive and intuit and creates an interpretation.

What about using the potential in the **future** to create my results?

That's what's beautiful about those souls who explore paths, who take them beyond the known past experiences. They have risked and tried something new. The inventors and innovators are our wayshowers.

> Each of us has this power.
> Each of us can invent.
> Each of us can release the past.
> Each of us can choose again.
> Each of us can rewire the brain.

I take the time to reflect and release the hold that past experiences have on me.

I trust in Universal Mind to "have my back."

I shift my view of life and declare Universal creativity as mine.

I am demonstrating results in my life, reflecting all that the Universe considers possible—all that will be.

DAY 10

The potential of the average person is like a huge ocean unsailed, a new continent unexplored, a world of possibilities waiting to be released and channeled toward some great good.
—*Brian Tracy*

I am guided by the same intelligence and inspired by the same imagination, which scatters the moon beams across the waves and holds the forces of nature in its grasp.
—*Ernest Holmes*

I picture the earth as a pale blue dot amid the multiple galaxies and physical universes.
It appears as a vessel navigating the infinite.
It is a miracle, dancing among the stars.
The universe has been evolving for fourteen billion years. What do the next fourteen billion years hold?
While intellectually I can conceive of something stretching out into eternity—somehow it's difficult to picture it, delimited as I am by the dimensions of this physical space. I feel bounded by the three dimensions and time.
AND! Time without end is the ultimate reality. Often I focus on that which I can see and that which science theorizes and proves. These four dimensions of time and space are familiar and comforting. What about the eleven dimensions postulated by string theory? The idea boggles the mind. By focusing on my knowledge of this material plane, it's possible to forget that Source creates all that is.
How can I reconnect with the Universal Creative Life Force?
Right now I let go of my earthly perceptions.
I place my faith in that which is the Truth of existence, of all beingness.
I center myself in the Divine Intelligence that expands infinity into eternity.
The same intelligence that guides the continuing evolution of all matter is pulsing through me.
We all reside in Infinity.
My potential is expressing for my highest good and the highest good of those around me.

I express my greatness effortlessly in each moment. I am in the flow.

DAY 11

The future is simply infinite possibility waiting to happen. What it waits on is human imagination to crystallize its possibility.

—Leland Kaiser

There is a power for good in the universe available to anyone and you can use this power for good in your life.

—Ernest Holmes

I claim the Universe's Power for good as my birthright.
I joyfully proclaim that good manifests in my life with ease.
I cocreate that which comes to be in the next hour, the next moment.
This day has never been. The future is a clean slate. I get to write my own life story.
I am a catalyst, a cocreator of that which is important to me.
I am Infinite possibility waiting to happen.
Where do I keep possibility waiting?
What can I do to ignite my imagination?
I see my dreams coming to life.
I see my walls, my barriers coming down. They were simply illusions.
Knowing that the mind is at work, materializing all my thoughts, what am I doing to get in touch with those driving needs playing hide-and-seek with my conscious, active mind?
What do I do to get in touch with the thoughts of which I'm unaware?
These thoughts create the results of my life by default.
The more I learn about myself, the more I am self-aware.
The more I objectively view the construct I call ego, the more my imagination aligns with the wishes of my heart and the power for good in the universe.
The more I let go, the more I manifest in ease.
I know that my attitudes, beliefs, and ideas create my judgments, which lead to my choices.
I choose to be aware.
I am consciously putting together that which is most important to me.

I joyfully activate my imagination.
I live in infinite possibility.

DAY 12

I didn't see it then, but it turned out that getting fired from Apple was the best thing that could have ever happened to me. The heaviness of being successful was replaced by the lightness of being a beginner again, less sure about everything. It freed me to enter one of the most creative periods of my life.

—Steve Jobs

The best way to arrive at the highest consciousness is to have a great faith in the willingness and the ability of Life to do all for us by working through us. We must believe in the inherent goodness and all-powerfulness of the Spirit of Truth.

—Ernest Holmes

Setbacks. Delays. Obstacles. Disappointments. Failures.

A heaviness of spirit comes over me, simply by reading these words—similar to what I feel when these situations occur. Thankfully, what I've come to understand is that these events are doorways to another dimension of my life.

It's important to acknowledge my feelings and the emotions when these do occur. I can take heart in knowing that the Universe is biased in my favor. I may not know exactly why I need to readjust my aim and my plans. I have faith that something, just as good or better, is being held for me in that creative field of potential that is Life!

In going from step one to a goal, course corrections are inevitable. Successes often require consistent modifications. Engineers of the first manned *Apollo* mission to the moon had a hard time fashioning a way to maintain an accurate trajectory. How could they send men to the moon, being off course 80 percent of the time?

When they changed their thinking—so that instead of trying to **stay** on course all the time, they focused on how to make constant small course corrections—they were successful. Apollo 11 was on course only 20 percent of the time, and still, they hit their target. Humans landed on the moon.

Off course, but on target!

Where can I make adjustments? Maybe even when my life is humming and thriving?

Life is dynamic. I am adapting. I flex.

I believe that the Universal creative process is right here, ready for me to make use of it.

**I am persistent in achieving my dreams. I am
one with the divine creative process.**

DAY 13

When nothing is sure, everything is possible.
—Margaret Drabble

A state of expectancy is a great asset; a state of uncertainty—
one moment thinking "perhaps" and the next moment think-
ing "I don't know"—will never get desired results.
—Ernest Holmes

Expectancy.
I love that word.
It connotes curiosity, excitement, joy, anticipation, enthusiasm, confidence, and surprise.
It means I am counting on something to occur with no expectation of what it looks like.
Dwelling in possibility is a lot like that.
It's having faith that good is on its way to me.
My day unfolds with a genuine thirst for discovering how my dreams are manifesting.
There have been times when this personal treasure hunt meant I came across something that didn't feel good.
When I look back on those events, I find something that is stirring.
Maybe they didn't feel good—AND maybe because of this feeling, I had enough dissatisfaction to do something different.
In the end, the upshot was that they brought me to my greater good.
I have learned to trust the Universe.
I now interpret these "not-feeling-so-good" times as turning points.
Because they were clearly what I did not want, contrast allowed me to focus more clearly on what I did want.

I choose joy and ease in manifesting my heart's desires.

DAY 14

Don't believe what your eyes are telling you. All they show is limitation. Look with your understanding, find out what you already know, and you'll see the way to fly.

—*Richard Bach*

Life is not just something to be endured. It is to be lived in joy, in a fullness without limit.

—*Ernest Holmes*

Power words!

When I use them, I am liberated from the constraints of the physical, and I soar into the heights of endless possibilities.

I am reminded that I am the universe, expressing in human form.

With that insight, my physical body changes—and in a flash, everything is new again.

I am attracting to me that which is most important to me. This is so—whether I am conscious of it or not. My thoughts create my reality. Neuroscience is affirming that my state of mind leads to my attitudes, which lead to my results. Sounds like something Buddha would say. I so appreciate that ancient wisdom clearly aligns with our contemporary science.

It is easy to see and feel that power words are genuinely potent.

I see myself manifesting in ease.

I am joy!

I am wisdom!

I am harmony!

I am courage!

I am love!

I am brilliant!

I am worthy!

I am capable!

I am all this and more!

I am an expression of the eternal life cycle.

I have always been, and I always will be.

I am ablaze like a star.

I celebrate me.

**I am powerful. I see with my inner essence. I
am potential—manifesting as me.**

DAY 15

Look for the opportunities in the difficulties, not the difficulties in the opportunities.

—*Victor Fiorelli*

Life is ever giving of Itself. We must receive, utilize and extend the gift. Success and prosperity are spiritual attributes belonging to all people.

—*Ernest Holmes*

I have the power!
I am a child of the Universe.
Sometimes I find myself asking: "Why do bad things happen to good people?"
It's especially hard when those things I call *bad* happen to me.
When I tune in to the life-giving energy that fuels all that is, I find this leads to other questions—no longer asking why something happened and instead asking, "How will I respond? What do I intend to do now that this happened?"
I have grown from those events.
I am renewed. I am not the same person after working through these.
I learn about myself and become more self-aware.
If I look at these situations as "feedback" or "dissonance," they point away from where I've been—they point to my future, where I'm going, focused on what my desire is.
I take steps that lead to the next segment of my life.
I thrive.
Life, truly, is ever giving of itself.
When I release judgments and dive into the glorious pool of infinite potential, I find I can let go of blame.
As I move forward, solutions become clearer.
With this clarity, I can focus my thoughts on the changes that I am seeking.
And Life wholeheartedly responds, "Yes!"
Possibility abounds!

Everywhere I turn, I see open doors.

DAY 16

Until one is committed, there is hesitancy, the chance to draw back, always ineffectiveness. Concerning all acts of initiative and creation, there is one elementary truth, the ignorance of which kills countless ideas and splendid plans: that the moment one definitely commits oneself, then providence moves too. All sorts of things occur to help one that would never otherwise have occurred. A whole stream of events issues from the decision, raising in one's favor all manner of unforeseen incidents, meetings and material assistance which no man could have dreamed would have come his way. Whatever you can do or dream you can, begin it. Boldness has genius, power, and magic in it. Begin it now.

—*Goethe*

Your soul belongs to the universe. Your mind is an outlet through which the Creative Intelligence of the Universe seeks fulfillment.

—*Ernest Holmes*

I am aware of my impulses, longings, and desires which accompany me in this life.

With this self-awareness, I can start my trek toward accepting my good.

Ernest Holmes says, "You may accept that the universe is filled with a Divine and Infinite Presence, perhaps the infinite of yourself. Not the infinite of your limited self, but the infinite of the Divine Self you must be. There must be a pattern of yourself in this invisible."

The mystics and philosophers through time have spoken of a Source of all that is.

Science affirms that all matter is energy.

This energy flows throughout the universe and individualizes as the person that I am.

I now set my sights for even greater fulfillment in all areas of my life.

I am a money magnet and can afford that which brings me joy and satisfaction.

My relationships flourish with the abundance of soul-to-soul intimacy and love.

I am healthier with each passing moment.

I know that my longings are Creation itself, urging me to discover my divinity.

I have faith that the right people and conditions are coming my way.

The Universe conspires in my favor.

I am in the flow of Creative Intelligence. Good comes to me naturally.

DAY 17

Some people see things as they are and say, "Why?" I dream things that never were and say, "Why not?"
— *George Bernard Shaw*

Life has entered into you and with it the irresistible impulse to create.

— *Ernest Holmes*

Why not?

Where do I allow universal expansion to flow through me naturally?

Where do I go along with any limits I have adopted?

Have I been deliberately creating, or have I been creating by default?

I know I've dreamed of attaining a goal, taking a fabulous trip, or making a major purchase, and "lo and behold," my dream manifests. My confidence builds. I am inspired to go for something else.

Every day I get in touch more and more with my belief of how I can grow. When I take a walk, I sometimes see a "green shoot" sprouting through concrete or a plant growing seemingly among rocks. Physical examples of that irresistible impulse to create.

I look up in the heavens, and I see stars that are no longer there and still their light beams on.

There are miracles everywhere I turn.

I reflect on my dreams, and I can see that they are waiting for me to catch up.

I take time to look at where I might be feeling resistance.

Am I too busy? Am I too tired?

What about all I have to do for those who expect something from me?

Are my priorities confused?

Are my "shoulds" conflicting with my "wants?"

Am I clear about the value I can gain?

I am ready to integrate into my core, what my heart tells me about my life's purpose.

I am a radiant being, shimmering with the impulse to create.

DAY 18

And once the storm is over, you won't remember how you made it through, how you managed to survive. You won't even be sure, whether the storm is really over. But one thing is certain. When you come out of the storm, you won't be the same person who walked in. That's what this storm's all about.

—Haruki Murakami

The most destructive force you and I have—and the most constructive—is our own unconscious emotional and thinking and feeling state.

—Ernest Holmes

This universe is expanding and evolving.
I am naturally expanding and evolving.
I am one with Universal Mind.
What a delectable feeling.
Regardless of my situations or conditions in this physical realm, the self-expression of Divine Intelligence through me, as me, is my truth.
When I face a bump in the road, it's easy to get stopped there. It's easy to judge myself as a failure for the role I played in the "problem." Easy to feel disheartened.
And then, a "BFO"—a blinding flash of the obvious.
I am expanding and evolving!
I choose to change my feelings of despondency.
I use my emotions as guides to what I want to manifest.
I can let go of judging myself as "less than."
I recenter myself in the knowing that "it is what it is."
I *cannot* rewrite history.
What I *can* do is get in touch again with what's important to me and I write a brand-new chapter. That empty page only looks blank—it actually holds the potential for a new creation.
The journey of my transformation is blessing me.
I am grateful that I am adaptable. I can change.

I create my preferred future in ease.

DAY 19

Start by doing what's necessary; then do what's possible; and suddenly you are doing the impossible.
— *St. Francis of Assisi*

We may stumble, but always, there is that eternal voice, forever whispering within our ear, that thing which causes the eternal quest, that thing which forever sings and sings.
— *Ernest Holmes*

"Doing the impossible."

That phrase in itself can sometimes stop me. Sometimes, it looks as if it's easier for someone else to have a breakthrough than it is for me. What's that about?

When I become aware of my "stuckness," it's like a red alert!

Where am I experiencing "red alerts?"

To change course, I take the time to ground myself in the knowing that, with deliberate intention, I can create something new, something different in my life.

I like doing this from a joyful place, a place of gratitude for all that I have, all that I am.

I personally continue to change and grow.

I can see that when I have a clear, focused thought, I manifest my heart's desire.

Sometimes it's like wizardry, and it happens really fast.

At other times, it's like tulips flowering. I can't see the blooms, and still, I am assured that the life process is at work.

I am comforted that, with a clear thought and a deliberate intention, I can start to do what's necessary, gain confidence by doing what's possible, and find myself doing what I had only thought was impossible.

I realize that Divine Intelligence is my ally.

In truth, I am one with the creative process of the universe.

The word *impossible* is powerless. It is simply a thought, and a thought can be changed.

I am thrilled knowing that with Divine Mind, all things are possible.

DAY 20

All of us were meant to be happy and successful. Life is more than a two-week vacation once a year. It is, and can be, exactly what you want it to be. There are no limits except those you put on yourself.

—*Thomas Willhite*

Life is greater than you have ever known it—the best is yet to come.

—*Ernest Holmes*

Happy and successful!
How can I attain greater and greater levels of happiness?

I see the joy in a child's smile,
> ...the full-bodied celebration of a frolicking puppy,
> ...the glow on a new mom's face,
> ...the sparkle in the eyes of two friends meeting.

I hear the fun in the laughter at a great joke,
> ...the excitement in someone sharing good news,
> ...the passion in an artist's song,
> ...the zeal in our teacher's lesson.

Happy thoughts zing through me. I am cheerful.
I'm available for the best that is yet to come.
I'm ready to go for my dreams!
I am more able to take risks when I feel "good."
Small risks. Big risks. It doesn't matter, as long as I move in the direction of my dreams.
I am guaranteed of success.
I am willing to step into my highest good, more and more, with each passing day.
I honor my innate longing to live more fully.

I am happy. I am successful. I am limitless.

DAY 21

When you throw everything up in the air, anything becomes possible.

—*Salman Rushdie*

It is done to you as you believe.

—*Ernest Holmes*

It's been said that "Life is a random series of events." This physical environment operates under laws of Chemistry and Physics that seemingly work that way. Somehow this randomness led to the specific principles that run my body. It doesn't look too random now.

Chaos creates order. Chaos creates.

Chaos in Physics is defined as the unpredictability inherent in a system, such as the weather, in which apparently random changes occur as a result of the system's extreme sensitivity to small differences in initial conditions. **It is said that an arbitrarily small disturbance of the current trajectory may lead to significantly different future behavior.** This sensitivity to initial conditions is popularly known as the "butterfly effect."

How can this be more believable than the knowing that one thought (an arbitrarily small disturbance) can change MY life's trajectory?

I say this "butterfly effect" is one indication that we, humans, are still neophytes, learning about the forces of the universe.

That "it is done as I believe" is a teaching that transcends time.

I choose to believe in myself, my power, my ability to rethink my future.

Am I leaning toward the abundance of my desire? Yes.

I look at my abundance, and I rejoice—for no matter what the appearances are, I am manifesting more and more in each moment.

More love. More forgiveness. More joy. More wisdom. More understanding. More money. More of life's gifts that bring satisfaction and renewal.

I accept that seemingly inconsequential events can lead me to my desired results.

Chaos can be scary.

When I see it as the doorway to splendid prospects, I breathe in Life, and I savor my good.

Chaos can work for me.

I know that beyond doubt and fear, there is something that blesses me.

DAY 22

Happiness, contentment, the health and growth of the soul, depend, as men have proved over and over again, upon some simple issue, some single turning of the soul.

—George A. Smith

Electricity was a reality in the universe when Moses led the children of Israel out of the land of Egypt. This is true of all-natural laws; they have always existed but only when understood may they be used.

—Ernest Holmes

The inception of the universe. The spontaneous surge of that energy that is all that is.

I like to think of that first flash as a divine spark. A divine spark that is never-ending.

It keeps going and going—boundless, ceaseless, interminable.

It is the divine spark of all creation.

It is the creative urging that drove energy to create matter to warp in time and space.

It led to planets, stars, galaxies, and **me**.

Somehow life emerged from a celestial body made of molten rocks, the earth we know.

This miraculous creation tells me again that all things are possible.

It conveys that these natural laws are here for me to understand and use.

Thought is the portal to that infinite dimension of original ideas that result in healing.

I have come into this world as an extension of Source energy.

This life-giving impulse wants me to consciously join this radiant, stunning dance of well-being.

Today I focus on well-being and health.

Do I judge it as "good," "the best," or "the worst?"

What matters is that in this moment, I envision a state of strength and vigor.

My body is in the here and now. It loves me, and I love it.

I take steps to enhance my feelings of well-being. I heal any area that is causing unease.

Any disease floats into nothingness as I allow more "ease" into my inner essence.

Every little cell in my body is happy.
Every little cell in my body is fine.
Every little cell in my body is tranquil.
Every little cell in my body is divine.

DAY 23

I must be willing to give up what I am in order to become what I will be.

—Albert Einstein

I see through all physical and mental obstructions to the one perfect Presence within me.

—Ernest Holmes

Grace…
Spoken with grace…
Forgiven with grace…
Provided a space of grace…
Filled with grace…
What does *grace* mean to me? Certainly more than kindness.
There seems to be a dimension of unconditional acceptance—
    one in which I am free to be.
It is soothing, calming, sacred.
It opens my empathetic heart.
It's about allowing.
Have I ever given myself the space of grace?
Have I spoken to that errant part of me with the grace of forgiveness?
Have I allowed myself to fully accept all of life's benevolence?
Right this minute, I cherish ME as never before!
I grant myself the grace to be exactly as I am in this flash of eternity.
I start from here.
I allow the dreams in my heart to speak to me, and I am grateful for my life's purpose.
I am ready.
I can let go of who I am to become that expression of me that brings more grace to life.
I release any obstacles and obstructions from my path.
The divine creative process is always here for me.
It works through me, as me.
And I give thanks!

I live in gratitude and grace.

DAY 24

Never tell me the sky's the limit when there are footprints on the moon.

—Unknown

We need only to say that our word is the law unto the case and calmly state what we want to be done, and then say and do nothing that contradicts it and wait for the fulfillment of that word. There is a power that operates on what we say, and it is done unto us, and we need have no fear about the results.

—Ernest Holmes

Businesses that are successful tell their story and relate how they started with a vision and how they set goals. The vision is as much about the product and service as it is about generating outcomes, e.g., community well-being, happiness, service, and more. Some examples are:

...we will add to life's enjoyment.

...adopt best practices with due care to the environment.

...be the number one advocate in the world for human worth.

...be the trusted resource for products that enhance home/family life.

These doctrines are the mainstay of business management programs. They are proven. And once a vision is declared, business people and organizations set about crafting goals with specific, measurable results and dates.

I find this quite exciting.

I see examples of the divine creative process in practical examples.

Somehow my brain wants reinforcement of my beliefs through "real-world" evidence.

What is my vision for myself?

Do I have goals? Am I tracking?

I realize that all my thoughts are overflowing with power!

As soon as I am clear on that which I want to be done, I can manifest results.

I align my emotions and feelings with my thoughts, and I am certain that my word is fulfilled.

I speak my word, and it is brought to pass.

DAY 25

In order to do what really matters to you, you have to, first of all, know what really matters to you.
—Dr. Edward Hallowell

We have within us a power that is greater than anything that we shall ever contact in the outer, a power that can overcome every obstacle in our life and set us safe, satisfied and at peace, healed and prosperous, in a new light, and in a new life. Mind, all mind, is right here. It is God's Mind, God's creative Power, God's creative Life.

—Ernest Holmes

Right now there is an endless stream of thoughts going through my brain.
Am I clear on what really matters to me?
Am I listening to my soul?
What is it telling me?
What have I been telling myself about my limitations?
Have I gotten in touch with my strengths?
What's really important is to look ahead.
Past experiences are history. I let them go. They are irrelevant.
What is my personal prophecy?
Who do I think I'm going to be?
What do I think I'm going to do?
Is this congruent with who I am right now and what I'm doing?
What stories am I telling about why I don't have something that is important to me?
Do I tell stories of how I'm winning in life?
Do I tell stories of how I've been disappointed?
Do I tell stories of my life's greatest moments?
Do I tell stories about my future possibilities?
These stories create my brain's maps.
I have the power within me to be at peace, to love, to be loved, to be safe, and to be healed.
Isn't this awesome?
Yea, me! Divine Mind and I are cocreating splendidness.

I already am what I seek.

DAY 26

Only he who attempts the absurd is capable of achieving the impossible.

—*Miguel de Unamuno*

It has taken humanity thousands of years to learn that it has the power to control its own destiny.

—*Ernest Holmes*

Is life happening to me? Or am I happening to life? Maybe it's not about either/or. When I tap into Life's Infinite Creative Process, I allow the wells of potential, that are the inner me, to activate, and the absurd is now ordinary. My personality—aka, my ego—has been constructed by life's experiences and by what people have told me about me.

"You're so bright."
"You're too tall."
"You're too practical."
"You're too ditzy."
"You're too young."
"You're too serious."
"You're such an achiever."
"You're not smart."
"You're spectacular."
"You're funny."
"You're so immature."
"You're so passionate."

These opinions and experiences create a map of myself. This feedback can lead to ideas that say, "They must be right. I guess that's who I am." I can start to believe that what I wish for is absurd.

Is it absurd to think that I am prosperous?

Is it absurd to think that I can have all that I dearly want?

Is it absurd to think that I am one with all of Life's energy?

Is it absurd to think that I am the person in charge of my destiny?

No! No! No! No! Even if in the moment I might see these and other so-called absurdities as impossible, I know I can change my mind.

I accept that my good is possible.

**My vision of what is possible is vast. My dream
is VERY reasonable and certain.**

63

DAY 27

It always seems impossible until it's done.
—*Nelson Mandela*

Wake up! Your word is all powerful. Your consciousness is one with Omnipotence. Your thought is infinite. Your destiny is eternal and your home is everlasting heaven. Realize the truth—I am living in a perfect universe, it always was perfect and always will be perfect.
—*Ernest Holmes*

There are times when I look at my circumstances and say, "I don't want this" and feel disappointed or disgruntled. I have been known to live in that space.
Now it has become easier to say, "Wow! What a moment of clarity."
By being aware of what I don't want, I can focus on what I DO want.
This focus is one of my greatest tools for manifesting my heart's desire.
I use it to set a clear intention for that which I choose to experience.
Next, I watch my self-talk and my feelings, matching them up positively with my goal.
I am on my way to deliberate creation.
I clear my mind of the trivial, physical conditions, and I connect with the Infinite.
The Infinite is all there is. I am astounded to know that eternity stretches, even between mathematical numbers—that decimal places can extend and extend and extend. What I see as solid and tangible in my day-to-day world is really only a speck of what is.
So what is my truth?
What ideas do I believe are right?
Do I have to always be right?
Can I be curious?
Maybe what my brain tells me is limited by what I have learned.
I can learn something new.

I believe in the power of my word. My thought is infinite.

DAY 28

Man often becomes what he believes himself to be. If I keep on saying to myself that I cannot do a certain thing, it is possible that I may end by really becoming incapable of doing it. On the contrary, if I have the belief that I can do it, I shall surely acquire the capacity to do it, even if I may not have it at the beginning.
—*Mahatma Gandhi*

There is a law of faith and belief which is just as definite as any other law in nature. This law utilizes the Creative Principle of Life in such a way that all lesser uses of It become submerged. This is the triumph of Spirit.
—*Ernest Holmes*

I can do it!
I think I can! I think I can! I think I can!
This is a great mantra for today.
A *mantra* is "a word or group of words that is considered capable of 'creating transformation.'" The spiritual interpretation of a mantra is regarded as a translation of the human will or desire into a form of action. It is a great tool for rewiring my brain—the neurons that fire together, wire together.
I know I can! I know I can! I know I can!
I imagine the feeling of power I attain if I repeat this the whole time I'm driving or grocery-shopping or cooking, or…
Brain scientists tell us that we are creating neural pathways all the time.
When we reuse the same thinking of yesterday, we create stronger neural pathways that grow into something akin to deep ruts.
Pretty soon my thoughts run along those "ruts" without conscious action on my part.
I become what I believe myself to be. I reframe my points of view.
I am utilizing the Creative Principle of Life! I allow myself to "rewire" to inspire!
I look at the results in my life and ask, "How can I change?"
I'm reminded of that old saying "If I always do what I've always done, I'll always get what I've always gotten."

My destiny is eternal. With a clear intention, I can do anything.

DAY 29

Seize this day, this moment. And if you choose to do the right thing now, if you just make a decision to try, then change begins. When the next moment comes, all you have to do is repeat that decision, maintain the course, and perseverance will take root and grow.

—*Patrice Gaines*

Man is surrounded by a great universal thought power which returns to him always just as he thinks. So plastic, so receptive is this mind, that it takes the slightest impression and molds it into conditions. Whatever is imaged is brought forth from mind into manifestation.

—*Ernest Holmes*

This is my day!
This is my life!
I surrender to Infinite Divine Mind and allow the good that is already mine to saturate my thoughts, and I trust that it is so.
Infinity is the basic nature of the Universe.
The nature of "all that is" is to expand and evolve.
It all started with that initial flicker we call "The Big Bang."
It gave rise to the energy that **is** all that is.
I am in the flow of all creation. I can feel it!
Each day I awaken to a new day—a day that has never been before. I rejoice!
When I see the sun shine and dazzle with its brilliance, I celebrate!
When the raindrops speak to me across my windowpane, I am in awe!
When the stars sparkle above, I know I am timeless!
I am in the flow of all creation.
In many ways, I am that toddler that discovered mud for the first time.
I am that teenager who knew absolutely everything.
I am that person that was in this form last year.
AND I am reborn each day.

I persevere, and I become the person of my dreams.

DAY 30

Life is simple. Everything happens for you, not to you. Everything happens at exactly the right moment, neither too soon nor too late. You don't have to like it…it's just easier if you do.

—Byron Katie

You belong to the universe in which you live; you are one with the Creative Genius back of this vast array of ceaseless motion, this original flow of life. You are as much a part of it as the sun, the earth and the air.

—Ernest Holmes

There are times when I think that the flow of the life-giving energy lies outside of me, that someone out there will gift it to me.
Happily it comes to me in a split second, that this is an error thought.
I know that I am a child of the universe.
I am one with that Creative Intelligence of the universe.
I know that the universe is always working in my favor.
So where does this thinking come from? The idea that things happen TO me? Seriously?
I don't have to know the answer to that question to acknowledge that all things that happen, bless me!
From victim to victor!
From tragedy to triumph!
Everything that transpires is neutral until I give it meaning.
I revel in my life's dance.
I see the probability in every circumstance, and I choose to have it be sacred.
I see possibility in taking the next step from where I am right now.
I am a proactive cocreator of my good, regardless of appearances.
Conditions are only feedback on where I am.
They serve to have me focus my attention on my good so I can stay the course or tack into the universal winds.

I am living the good life and loving every minute!

DAY 31

You do not need to know precisely what is happening, or exactly where it is all going. What you need is to recognize the possibilities and challenges offered by the present moment, and to embrace them with courage, faith and hope.
—*Thomas Merton*

The whole world, from the least to the greatest, must know the truth so that man may understand the great laws that govern his life. He must learn to control his own destiny, to heal his own body and bring happiness to his own soul.
—*Ernest Holmes*

A navigational system or global positioning system (GPS) is quite a marvel. Once I set a destination, the system tells me where to turn, what exit to take, and sometimes, how long the trip will take. If, for any reason, I need to stop or make an unexpected turn, it will alert me to the fact that I'm deviating from my original plan.

It's great!

It reminds me that the divine creative process is akin to that.

Starting with a clear sense of purpose, a goal, a dream, a vision, Divine Intelligence guides me as I step into manifestation.

Neuroscience tells us that the brain, with its cognitive imperative, works to make sense of what's mine to do. It does so based on what it knows. As I feed it with thoughts that are congruent with what I say I want, it "rewires" to match my desires. When my actions are incongruent with those purposeful beliefs, my results are clear indicators that I have shifted from my course.

Something else that happens with a GPS is that if I'm going someplace I've never been to at night, to a location with no street lamps and roads that are unfamiliar to me, I can feel anxiety at not knowing exactly where I am. Then I remember! My GPS knows. I trust my system.

So it is with the Universal Life-giving Energy. Trusting that the Creator is there for me always, I can move into spaces where I may not know precisely where things are going. I remember! Infinite Mind knows. I trust my system divine. I am firm in my belief that all the power of the Spirit is working through my thought as I believe and receive.

**I enjoy exploring life's many wonderful possibilities,
manifesting what is mine to be.**

DAY 32

We all shine on...like the moon and the stars and the sun...
we all shine on...come on and on and on...

—*John Lennon*

Perfect peace to the soul, as we rest in the realization of our
unity with all there is, was, or ever will be. One with Infinite
Mind. All the power of the Spirit is working through our
thought, as we believe and receive.

—*Ernest Holmes*

Every day I am growing my strength of belief in the magnificence that is
who I am!

I am a channel for the divine expression of life as me.

That life-giving energy is flowing all the time—evolving and expanding—
creating something more than what was there yesterday.

We know the physical universe is expanding—we can see it pulling away
through our awe-inspiring telescopes.

This forward motion draws me into that current of possibility every second.

My physical form is quite enthralled with this earthly plane.

It likes to think that this realm of time and space is real.

After all, the brain is a tremendous navigator, and to do a good job, it must
make sense of the sensory information it receives.

I find it fascinating that eyes are merely capturing shapes and lines.

My brain takes all this and "fabricates" information based on what it knows.

I see why it has to "define" this series of happenings as "reality."

It serves as an anchor—much like gravity—defining me in its dialect.

I am so much more than the person filling up this space.

I am an Infinite being. Immortality is my true nature.

The Universal Truth about life is that life never ends.

What we call death is simply the changing of one form of life for another.

Death, the belief and perception that life must come to an end, is a human
concept.

I am an extension of Infinite Source Energy.

DAY 33

If you want to know your past—look into your present conditions.
If you want to know your future—look into your present actions.

—Chinese Proverb

There is a Power around you that knows and that understands all things. This Power works like the soil; it receives the seed of your thought and at once begins to operate upon it. It will receive whatever you give to it and will create for you and throw back at you whatever you think into it.

—Ernest Holmes

Am I reactive or proactive?
A thermometer reacts to the environment.
A thermostat creates the environment.
Which am I?
I know that I am one with Divine Mind, the all-pervasive creative power.
I take back my power.
What do I say I want to do?
What am I doing?
Are these matching "mind-sets?"
Are my actions aligned with what I say I want?
The step I take today sets my course for my future.
I can do so with awareness, consciously or out of default.
When I'm unclear or confused, it can feel like hard work.
Right now I tap into that inner wisdom, and I call up that clarity of purpose.
And the ease of flowing with the currents in the river of life, instead of struggling to go upstream, provides the oomph I need to do what I say I want to do.
This Divine Intelligence is the truth of who I am.
My present actions are bringing to me that which is mine to experience.
Life is marvel-filled! I am one with all that is and all that will be.

I am a proactive cocreator of my life divine!

DAY 34

The miracle is not to fly in the air, or to walk on the water, but to walk on the earth.

—*Chinese Proverb*

Your soul belongs to the universe. Your mind is an outlet through which the Creative Intelligence of the universe seeks fulfillment.

—*Ernest Holmes*

Miracles are everywhere.

When I think of the formation of planet Earth fourteen billion years ago—from atoms and subatomic particles bouncing into each other—I know I am treading on a miracle.

I know that there were only rocks and water at the onset.

How did that first one-celled organism come to be? That was definitely a miracle.

Now, fast-forward a few million years and that one-celled organism "permutated" into the diverse life forms we see today. That series of growth spurts was like millions of miracles expanding and evolving as the universe continues its journey into infinity.

Then there's the miracle of the human body! I know I'm not the only one who marvels at the magnificence of the anatomy, the intelligent workings of the brain and mind, the mystery of its physical systems, and the differentiation of every individual cell according to its purpose.

Who am I to doubt that this universe I grew up learning about actually has sibling universes?

I am grounded in my faith that this creative life force is not done yet. It is eternal.

It continues to create and evolve everything and everyone that is currently here and all that exists in this and other universes—beings and things we have not yet met.

I love this unfoldment of glories.

It is a breathtaking time to be alive.

**I am one with the inventive Divine Genius.
I am evolving. I am a miracle.**

DAY 35

All the possibilities of your human destiny are asleep in your soul. You are here to realize and honor these possibilities. When love comes in to your life, unrecognized dimensions of your destiny awaken and blossom and grow. Possibility is the secret heart of time.

—*John O'Donohue*

Through the door of our own thoughts, we enter into the Universal Consciousness, into a complete realization of life and truth, of love and beauty, and as we sit in the silence of our own souls and listen, it will be the greatest thing that we ever do. We realize that we are One with Cause.

—*Ernest Holmes*

For thousands of years, the *law of cause and effect* guided scientific inquiry. It is the dominant principle of classical physics.

I can see that it was a reasonable corollary to see this principle at work in the actions of Divine Intelligence.

After all, the cosmos is Universal Consciousness and has intelligence, purpose, beauty, and order.

I know that all that is, is one with Divine Mind, the Universal Creative Spirit.

The Law of Cause and Effect is always at work.

This law simply states that every action has a consequence—creative, destructive, or neutral.

The Law of Attraction is one aspect of that law.

I do believe that all the possibilities of my human destiny lie in my inner being—my soul.

These possibilities are endless—for Universal Consciousness, the Source of all, is working through me, as me.

I have merely to focus my attention on that which is important to me and clear my thoughts of any opposing beliefs.

This declaration is the cause. The effect will naturally follow.

What a joy!

I am one with Cause, and all is well.

DAY 36

*If the only prayer you said in your whole life was "thank you,"
that would suffice.*

—Meister Eckhart

*As consciousness grows, it will manifest in enlarged oppor-
tunities and a greater field of action. Feel that you are surrounded by all the power that there is when you speak and
never doubt but that what you say will spring into being.*

—Ernest Holmes

Each day brings a field of promise.

It has never existed before, and it will never be again.

It is ripe, with an array of choices that are mine to make.

I am grateful for the immeasurable bounty of me.

My brain thrives with thanksgiving.

When I am grateful, I am nurturing my genius and talents.

It is the lubricant that facilitates my rushing in ease with the Universal
Force.

When I am in appreciation of what is going on in my life, more good flows
my way.

It's as if expressing my gratitude somehow "seals the deal."

Gratitude is a power. It transforms consciousness. It is a healing, creative
energy.

Gratitude is both a magnet for what I want and a channel for my circula-
tion of good.

Gratitude is a blessing.

As I cultivate it more and more, I feel I can be, do, and have anything.

Gratitude is an attitude that connects me to the Source.

The more grateful I am, the easier it is to connect with the Creator.

With gratitude I activate the energy of imagination and destiny.

When I am thankful for seeing my desire manifesting in thought, in my
mind, I send out a wave of faith and certainty that this will come to pass.

The Universe "senses" my feeling of completion.

And it is done unto me, as I believe.

My thoughts paint my desired, remarkable future!

DAY 37

Never say that you can't do something, or that something seems impossible, or that something can't be done, no matter how discouraging or harrowing it may be; human beings are limited only by what we allow ourselves to be limited by: our own minds. We are each the masters of our own reality; when we become self-aware to this: absolutely anything in the world is possible.

—*Mike Norton*

The principle of all life…we are surrounded by a thinking medium from which all things come. We think into it; it does the rest…. Our ability to attract will depend upon the largeness of our thought as we feel that it flows out into a great Universal Creative Power.

—*Ernest Holmes*

I give up "struggle" thinking.

Sometimes I feel as if all is splendid in my world! I go from win to win to win. It's simply extraordinary.

And then there are times when things aren't going as I planned.

These are important times. My emotions are giving me data, pointers.

I honor my sentiments and allow myself to feel how significant this is for me.

Then I step into possibility thinking, grateful for the opportunity to learn that I can find some "golden nugget" in the situation.

First, I am aware enough that I can recognize the discord; I recognize when I'm off course. That's good news, and I am grateful.

Second, I get clear feedback on how I might need to adapt my plans. It's possible I might have to change my actions to course-correct so that I stay on track to reach my target. This feedback allows me to clarify my area of concentration. Thank you, Universe.

Third, I recognize that the answer or solution is always within me. Personal responsibility is my gift to me. It means I have the "ability to respond." I get to decide to focus on my next steps rather than lingering on wanting to change history. I appreciate my self-care.

The struggle becomes my "alarm" system, telling me I've got choices to make.

I am empowered! I can move on!

I move forward with grace and ease. Anything is absolutely possible for me.

DAY 38

Look beyond the moment. Send your thoughts out on a shaft of faith into tomorrow where the full meaning of today becomes apparent.

—*Jack Boland*

But you are an individual, like all other individuals, gradually awakening to the greater possibility. If Life made you out of Itself, which It most certainly did, and if you are an individual just a little different from all other individuals who ever lived, then Life not only created you as an independent being, It also implanted a unique something within you.

—*Ernest Holmes*

Who am I now?
It is impossible to be the same person I was an hour ago.
I have expanded and evolved along with all Universal Creations.
I have new information.
I have done things—planned and unplanned—that led to certain, new results.
My future is so bright it dazzles!
Am I ready to step further into my greatness?
What do I need to release?
Am I living from my soul's purpose, or from a sphere of resentments?
Am I embracing the abundance of the Universe, or am I buying into the scarcity illusion?
What can I let go of so that I am lighter and have greater clarity?
What can I embrace that lifts me to my "crow's nest" so that I view infinite possibility?
Am I being the person I truly want to be?
Do I want to be healthier, wealthier, happier, better at my job, or be a better friend?
What do I want to be? What do I want to do? What do I want to have?
Be. Do. Have.
With clarity of what's important to me, I can BE with authenticity.
This expression of "me" will transform my experiences so that I DO what is necessary to attract what I want to HAVE.
I can start now, right from where I am.

I am a unique creation, swimming in the pool of infinite possibility.

DAY 39

Nobody knows how things will turn out, that's why they go ahead and play the game... You give it your all and sometimes amazing things happen, but it's hardly ever what you expect.

—Gennifer Choldenko

Heaven and earth will pass away but my word will accomplish. In calm confidence and perfect faith, speak and wait upon the perfect law. Get that mental attitude that never wavers. Be sure and it will be done.

—Ernest Holmes

To try.

I've heard that famous quote of Yoda's: "Do or do not. There is no try."

I understand the sentiment for driving toward action and results.

AND I am grateful that sometimes, to get started, I've got to take that next step, even if I don't know exactly how things will turn out.

What will the next hour bring? The next day?

What is yet to transpire is all potential.

That next hour is overflowing with possibility.

It is what I make of it!

What a concept! The beginning in the end. The end in the beginning.

When I remember that infinity is the basic nature of the Universe, I am more able to keep my eyes on the horizon—looking forward. The nature of "all that is" is to create. It all started with that infinite burst of energy from seemingly nothing. It keeps unfolding into eternity.

Again and again, I am reminded that everything starts with me!

My thoughts, attitudes, and beliefs are mapping my life's journey.

I am writing the next chapter of my life.

That next hour is a blank sheet, awaiting the indelible ink of my thoughts and actions.

I own my future!

I am the source of my fulfillment.

DAY 40

The possible's slow fuse is lit by the Imagination. I dwell in possibility.

—Emily Dickinson

You belong to the universe in which you live, you are one with the Creative Genius back of this vast array of ceaseless motion, this original flow of life. You are as much a part of it as the sun, the earth and the air. There is something in you telling you this—like a voice echoing from some mountain top of inward vision, like a light whose origin no man has seen, like an impulse welling up from an invisible source.

—Ernest Holmes

I am thrilled that within me is the power to light the fuse of possibility.
I belong to the universe in which I live!
I am one with the Creative Genius back of this vast array of ceaseless motion.
I am imagination in this human form.
When I took that first baby step—walking came from my imagination.
When I spoke that first word—speech came from my imagination.
I was born with a brain and physiology that responded to my faith, my ideas.
I didn't even know *then* what this "cocreation something" was all about.
Now I know.
How can I consider that what was true when I first started navigating the world is not operational anymore? Of course, it is.
Everything is created twice—once in mind, and then in reality.
I have problem-solving skills. That's my imagination at work.
I can plan a vacation or a creative "staycation." That's my imagination at play.
I can put together a framework for making my contribution through my work and vocation. That's my imagination succeeding.
I delight in knowing that imagination is an innate power, standing at the ready to support me.
All things are possible.
The divine creative process sustains and fuels me.
There is no mystery in my history. It is teeming with joy. I am grateful for all the good I manifest. Continuously.

"I dwell in possibility." Yes!

ABOUT THE AUTHOR

Hispana. Student. Scientist. Executive. Breast Cancer Survivor. Alive. Miracles. Abundance. Radiance.

Linda Villegas Bremer is grateful she grew up in a Mexican enclave in Texas. She grew up in a culture immersed in mysticism and spirituality. *Curanderos* and shape-shifters were taken for granted. Then she majored in chemistry and spent years in the field of information technology. She is thrilled that neuroscience, quantum physics, and inclusive spiritual lessons stretch our horizon of possibility. She is a fan of what Neuroscience reminds us: that "our thoughts become things."

"Change your thoughts—change your life."—Wayne Dyer

CPSIA information can be obtained
at www.ICGtesting.com
Printed in the USA
BVHW030841260720
584579BV00001B/62